This Book
Belongs To:

_____

Of Words

Words are what gives structure to our writing!

Having the words, using the words.

For WITHOUT WORDS THERE IS NO STORY, WITHOUT WORDS THERE IS NO WRITING!

Learn a word or two or three, a day and use it in every way, building your vocabulary.

1st New Word_____

Write meaning in box below

2nd New Word_____

Write meaning in box below

3rd New Word_____

Write meaning in box below

Bringing Out the Potential of Children Writers/Authors

****

Workbook & Ideas Journal

Bringing Out the Potential of Children. Writers/Authors

Workbook
with an
Ideas Journal

ISBN978-1-7751178-5-8

Cover Design: Patrice Porter

Words

Learn a word or two or three, a day and use it in every way, building your vocabulary.

1st New Word_____

Write meaning in box below

2nd New Word_____

Write meaning in box below

3rd New Word_____

Write meaning in box below

Words

Learn a word or two or three, a day and use it in every way, building your vocabulary.

1st New Word_____

Write meaning in box below

2nd New Word_____

Write meaning in box below

3rd New Word_____

Write meaning in box below

Words

Learn a word or two or three, a day and use it in every way, building your vocabulary.

1st New Word_____

Write meaning in box below

2nd New Word_____

Write meaning in box below

3rd New Word_____

Write meaning in box below

Words

Learn a word or two or three, a day and use it in every way, building your vocabulary.

1st New Word_____

Write meaning in box below

2nd New Word_____

Write meaning in box below

3rd New Word_____

Write meaning in box below

Words

Learn a word or two or three, a day and use it in every way, building your vocabulary.

1st New Word_____

Write meaning in box below

2nd New Word_____

Write meaning in box below

3rd New Word_____

Write meaning in box below

Words

Learn a word or two or three, a day and use it in every way, building your vocabulary.

1st New Word_____

Write meaning in box below

2nd New Word_____

Write meaning in box below

3rd New Word_____

Write meaning in box below

Words

Learn a word or two or three, a day and use it in every way, building your vocabulary.

1st New Word_____

Write meaning in box below

2nd New Word_____

Write meaning in box below

3rd New Word_____

Write meaning in box below

Words

Learn a word or two or three, a day and use it in every way, building your vocabulary.

1st New Word_____

Write meaning in box below

2nd New Word_____

Write meaning in box below

3rd New Word_____

Write meaning in box below

Words

Learn a word or two or three, a day and use it in every way, building your vocabulary.

1st New Word_____

Write meaning in box below

2nd New Word_____

Write meaning in box below

3rd New Word_____

Write meaning in box below

Words

Learn a word or two or three, a day and use it in every way, building your vocabulary.

1st New Word_____

Write meaning in box below

2nd New Word_____

Write meaning in box below

3rd New Word_____

Write meaning in box below

Words

Learn a word or two or three, a day and use it in every way, building your vocabulary.

1st New Word_____

Write meaning in box below

2nd New Word_____

Write meaning in box below

3rd New Word_____

Write meaning in box below

Words

Learn a word or two or three, a day and use it in every way, building your vocabulary.

1st New Word_____

Write meaning in box below

2nd New Word_____

Write meaning in box below

3rd New Word_____

Write meaning in box below

Words

Learn a word or two or three, a day and use it in every way, building your vocabulary.

1st New Word_____

Write meaning in box below

2nd New Word_____

Write meaning in box below

3rd New Word_____

Write meaning in box below

Developing The Power Of Observation

Train Yourself To Take In All You Are Experiencing

For ALL Information is Important at some time!

Exercise to develop your power of observation :
Walk into a room or place you know. Exit that room or place and write in the box below every thing you remember about that room or place. Include as much detail as possible

Exercise to develop your power of observation (continued): Now return to that same room or place Focus only on what you can remember in this exercise. That is what we will be working to strengthen. On returning to that same room or place see what other details to that room and place there are. Write them in the box below

Exercise to develop your power of observation (continued): Once you have been working on building your power of observation for awhile try repeating this exercise. Try it again in the same place then try it in a new area.

Repeat exercise returning to the original place for a quick visit.

Write your observations in the box below

Exercise to develop your power of observation (continued):

Once you have been working on building your power of observation for awhile return to this new area once

Check the development of your power of observation and write what your new observations are in the box below

Exercise to develop your power of observation #3

Write down 3 Major Observations of your day...

1st Main Observation _____

_____

_____

_____

_____

_____

2nd Major Observation _____

_____

_____

_____

_____

_____

3rd Major Observation _____

_____

_____

_____

_____

_____

Book Title Brainstorming

5 Titles I liked from my research of titles in my niche/genre on Amazon

* 1 _____

_____

_____

*2 _____

_____

_____

*3 _____

_____

_____

*4 _____

_____

_____

*5 _____

_____

_____

Title Brainstorming Ideas – Write them in here

Book Title Ideas

Share your book title ideas with friends and family perhaps they will have some ideas for you too!

My friend's choice from my book title ideas

_____

_____

_____

My family's choice from my book title ideas

_____

_____

_____

NOTES

Opening Paragraphs

It's the beginning that hooks your reader in – grabs their interest to keep them turning the pages

Research the opening sentence/paragraphs from famous authors to model after

1st **Author's name and book**_____

_____

Write the opening paragraph in box below

2nd **Author's name and book**_____

_____

Write the opening paragraph in box below

3rd **Author's name and book**_____

_____

Write the opening paragraph in box below

Opening Paragraphs

Have a good beginning to your book, a good middle and a good end of your book. Something that keeps your readers wanting to turn the pages and keep on reading your work.

Let's work on your "Hook" for a good beginning.

Share them with your friends and family mark their response below each "Hook" idea

Hook Idea #1_____

_____

_____

_____

Did this hook capture my friends and families interest?

__Yes

__ No

If no, what are the reasons why it never caught their attention. Enter them in the box below.

Opening Paragraphs

Hook Idea #2_____

_____

_____

_____

Did this hook capture my friends and families interest?

__Yes

__ No

If no, what are the reasons why it never caught their attentions. Enter them in the box below.

Opening Paragraphs

Hook Idea #3_____

_____

_____

_____

Did this hook capture my friends and families interest?

__Yes

__ No

If no, what are the reasons why it never caught their attentions. Enter them in the box below.

Outlining My Book

Have a process to keep focused and keep control of the direction of your book.

You can write out an outline of your book or use a mind map. Go ahead and enter your ideas in the mind map below.

Outlining My Book

Example of writing out an outline is to work from a table of content for what would be included in your book. Go ahead and fill in the blanks to fit in your content.

Table of Contents

Chapter 1 Title _____

_____

_____

Chapter 2 Title_____

_____

_____

Chapter 3 Title_____

_____

_____

Chapter 4 Title_____

_____

_____

Chapter 5 Title_____

_____

_____

Outlining My Book

Example of writing out an outline (continued) Write out what would be included in your book in the format as below. Go ahead and fill in the blanks to fit in your content.

Chapter 1 Title

In This Chapter We're Talking About (Enter in CHAPTER TITLE).

Bullet point first part of content

Bullet point 2nd part of content

Bullet point 3rd part of content

To summarize this beginning chapter

In this Chapter we Learned how to (insert CHAPTER TITLE)

The next chapter we'll be covering how to NEXT (Insert CHAPTER TITLE).

Outlining My Book

Example of writing out an outline for your book (continued)

Chapter 2 Title

In This Chapter We're Talking About (Enter in CHAPTER TITLE).

Bullet point first part of content

Bullet point 2nd part of content

Bullet point 3rd part of content

To summarize this beginning chapter

In this Chapter we Learned how to (insert CHAPTER TITLE)

The next chapter we'll be covering how to NEXT (Insert CHAPTER TITLE).

Outlining My Book

Example of writing out an outline for your book (continued)

Chapter 3 Title

In This Chapter We're Talking About (Enter in CHAPTER TITLE).

Bullet point first part of content

Bullet point 2nd part of content

Bullet point 3rd part of content

To summarize this beginning chapter

In this Chapter we Learned how to (insert CHAPTER TITLE)

The next chapter we'll be covering how to NEXT (Insert CHAPTER TITLE).

Outlining My Book

Example of writing out an outline for your book (continued)

Chapter 4 Title

In This Chapter We're Talking About (Enter in CHAPTER TITLE).

Bullet point first part of content

Bullet point 2nd part of content

Bullet point 3rd part of content

To summarize this beginning chapter

In this Chapter we Learned how to (insert CHAPTER TITLE)

The next chapter we'll be covering how to NEXT (Insert CHAPTER TITLE).

Outlining My Book

Example of writing out an outline for your book (continued)

Chapter 5 Title

In This Chapter We're Talking About (Enter in CHAPTER TITLE).

Bullet point first part of content

Bullet point 2nd part of content

Bullet point 3rd part of content

To summarize this beginning chapter

In this Chapter we Learned how to (insert CHAPTER TITLE)

The next chapter we'll be covering how to NEXT (Insert CHAPTER TITLE).

Book Endings

It's the ending, which is what your reader leaves with – here's your chance for making a real impact!

Research the endings from famous authors to model after

1st Author's name and book_____

_____

Write the ending in box below

2nd Author's name and book_____

_____

Write the ending in box below

Book Endings

Brainstorm some book endings and write them below.

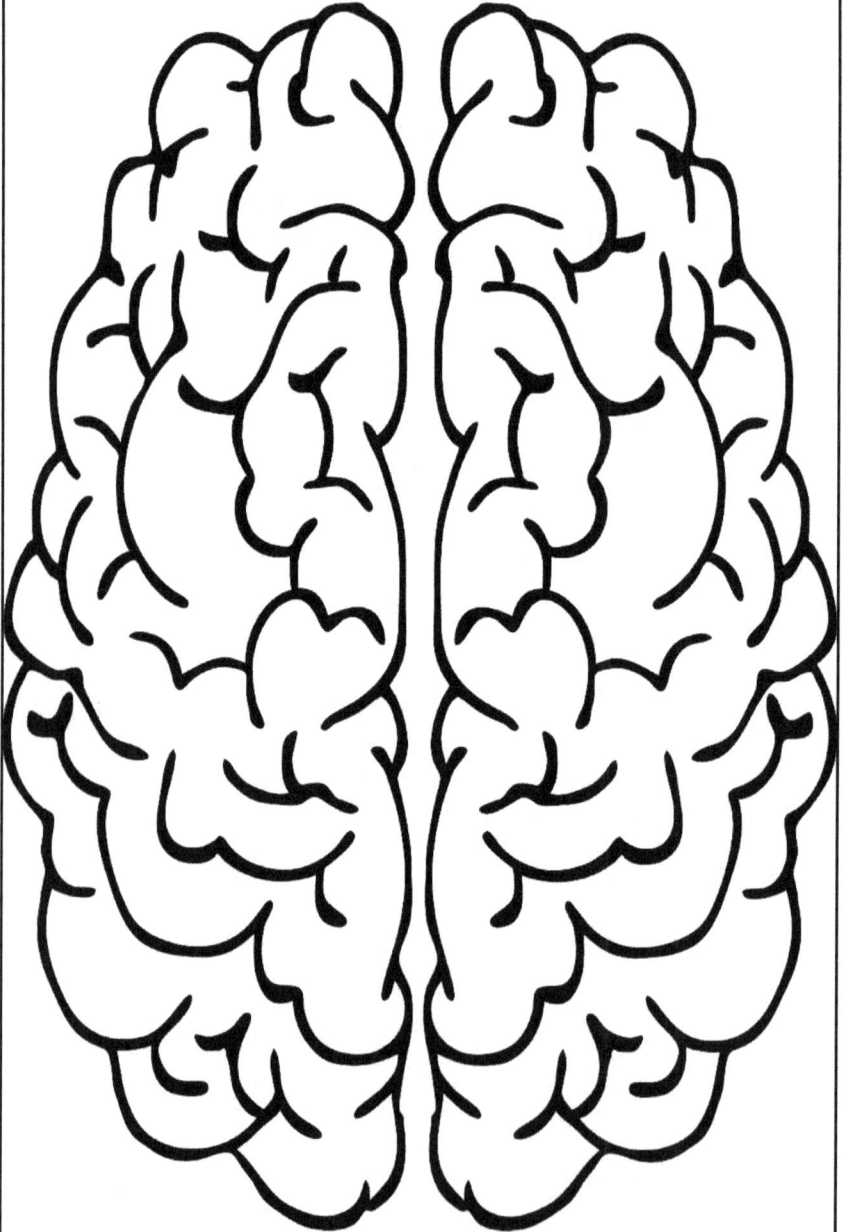

Book Endings

Brainstorm some book endings and write them below.

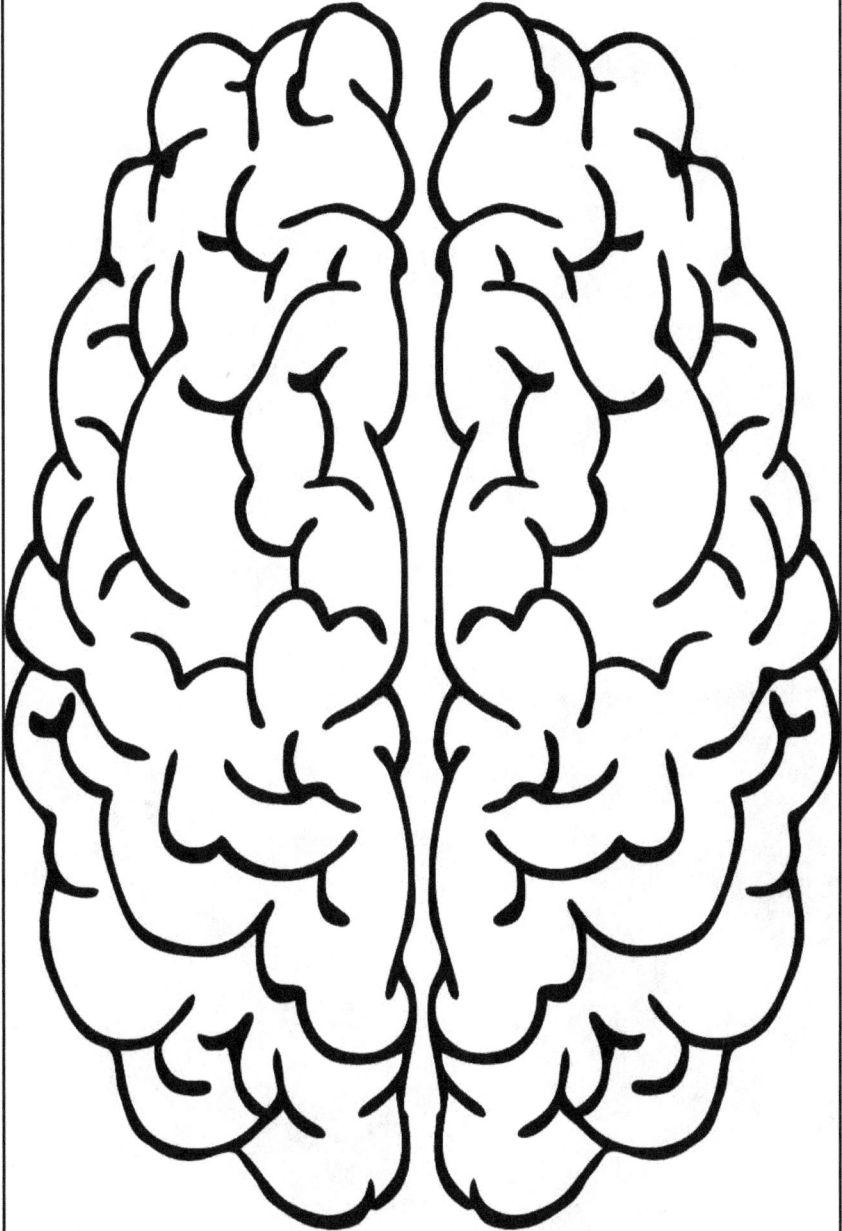

My Ideas

When your ideas come to you write them down.
Have notepads all over the place ready just for this.

"The best way to have a good idea is to have a lot of ideas~ Dr. Linus Pauling

My ideas

_____

_____

_____

_____

_____

_____

_____

_____

_____

_____

_____

_____

_____

_____

_____

_____

My ideas

_____

_____

_____

_____

_____

_____

_____

_____

_____

_____

_____

_____

_____

_____

_____

_____

> *"You have within you the strength, the patience, and the passion to reach for the stars to change the world."* ~ *Harriet Tubman*

My ideas

_____

_____

_____

_____

_____

_____

_____

_____

_____

_____

_____

_____

_____

_____

_____

_____

My ideas

_____

_____

_____

_____

_____

_____

_____

_____

_____

_____

_____

_____

_____

_____

_____

_____

> *"Everyone is a genius at least once a year. The Real geniuses simply have their bright ideas closer together.~ George C. Lichtenberg*

My ideas

_____

_____

_____

_____

_____

_____

_____

_____

_____

_____

_____

_____

_____

_____

_____

_____

My ideas

_____

_____

_____

_____

_____

_____

_____

_____

_____

_____

_____

_____

_____

_____

_____

_____

> *"I can't understand why people are frightened of new ideas. I'm frightened of the old ones."* ~ John Cage

My ideas

_____
_____
_____
_____
_____
_____
_____
_____
_____
_____
_____
_____
_____
_____
_____
_____
_____
_____
_____
_____

My ideas

_____

_____

_____

_____

_____

_____

_____

_____

_____

_____

_____

_____

_____

_____

_____

_____

_____

"If at first the idea is not absurd, then there is no hope for it." ~ Albert Einstein

My ideas

_____

_____

_____

_____

_____

_____

_____

_____

_____

_____

_____

_____

_____

_____

_____

_____

_____

My ideas

_____

_____

_____

_____

_____

_____

_____

_____

_____

_____

_____

_____

_____

_____

_____

_____

_____

"Creativity is not the finding of a thing, but the making something out of it after it is found." ~James Russel Lowell

My ideas

_____

_____

_____

_____

_____

_____

_____

_____

_____

_____

_____

_____

_____

_____

_____

_____

_____

My ideas

_____

_____

_____

_____

_____

_____

_____

_____

_____

_____

_____

_____

_____

_____

_____

_____

"A mediocre idea that generates enthusiasm will go further than a great idea that inspires no one." ~
Mary Kay Ash

My ideas

_____
_____
_____
_____
_____
_____
_____
_____
_____
_____
_____
_____
_____
_____
_____
_____
_____

My ideas

"Great minds discuss ideas, average minds discuss events, small minds discuss people." ~ Eleanor Roosevelt

~

My ideas

_____
_____
_____
_____
_____
_____
_____
_____
_____
_____
_____
_____
_____
_____
_____
_____

My ideas

_____

_____

_____

_____

_____

_____

_____

_____

_____

_____

_____

_____

_____

_____

_____

_____

_____

_____

"The ability to convert ideas to things is the secret of outward success." ~ Henry Ward Beecher

My ideas

_____

_____

_____

_____

_____

_____

_____

_____

_____

_____

_____

_____

_____

_____

_____

_____

My ideas

_____

_____

_____

_____

_____

_____

_____

_____

_____

_____

_____

_____

_____

_____

_____

"When all think alike, then no one is thinking~ Walter Lippman

My ideas

_____

_____

_____

_____

_____

_____

_____

_____

_____

_____

_____

_____

_____

_____

_____

_____

_____

My ideas

_____

_____

_____

_____

_____

_____

_____

_____

_____

_____

_____

_____

_____

_____

_____

_____

> *"Ideas can be life changing. Sometimes all you need to open the door is just one more good idea."*
> *~Jim Rohn*

My ideas

_____

_____

_____

_____

_____

_____

_____

_____

_____

_____

_____

_____

_____

_____

_____

_____

My ideas

_____

_____

_____

_____

_____

_____

_____

_____

_____

_____

_____

_____

_____

_____

_____

_____

_____

_____

"When all think alike, then no one is thinking~ Walter Lippman

My ideas

_____

_____

_____

_____

_____

_____

_____

_____

_____

_____

_____

_____

_____

_____

_____

_____

_____

My ideas

_____

_____

_____

_____

_____

_____

_____

_____

_____

_____

_____

_____

_____

_____

_____

_____

My ideas

_____

_____

_____

_____

_____

_____

_____

_____

_____

_____

_____

_____

_____

_____

_____

_____

_____

www.ingramcontent.com/pod-product-compliance
Lightning Source LLC
Chambersburg PA
CBHW071932020426
42331CB00010B/2834